A Tennis Love Story

Sue Huffman Stanley

authorHOUSE®

AuthorHouse™
1663 Liberty Drive, Suite 200
Bloomington, IN 47403
www.authorhouse.com
Phone: 1-800-839-8640

First published by AuthorHouse 5/11/2009

ISBN: 978-1-4389-3232-3 (sc)
ISBN: 978-1-4389-3233-0 (hc)

Printed in the United States of America
Bloomington, Indiana

This book is printed on acid-free paper.

To my children, who have gone through this journey with me, whom I love with all my heart.

To tennis players all over the world who allow the sport of tennis to bring joy, happiness, and love into their lives. To everyone who realizes that our Savior, the Lord Jesus Christ, can help us get through any crisis if we turn our hearts to Him, and allow Him to do it.

INTRODUCTION

Read the story of how a young girl at the age of thirteen, who loves tennis, meets a young man age seventeen on a tennis court and **A Tennis Love Story** evolves. One thing leads to another until tennis becomes their everyday outing event. It is a beautiful love story. The story illustrates how the Lord kept them together utilizing the sport of tennis in such a magnificent way.

The story includes finishing high school, college, having three babies, and obtaining a master's degree, while all the time tennis being a common thread. There are always trials, but their love for one another and the Lord always manage to get them through.

Through the courtship and marriage, many events happen that lead up to an untimely casualty. This is devastating and definitely a life changing event. Through the grace of God

Sue was carried on in life. It is a charming love story, full of joy and some sorrows, yet ends in wonderful memories and honor to a good man, a super tennis player, a wonderful dad, and a loving husband.

A TENNIS LOVE STORY

When I was a small child, I always wanted to play with my father, Paul Butcher. It was that father/daughter thing where opposites attract, and daddies are always gentle and loving with their daughters. He always made my sisters and me laugh and enjoy the simple life, because back in the fifties we didn't have a lot of money. It didn't matter. I just remember all the fun I had with my dad.

By the time I was nine, in 1957, I came to know the Lord in a real way. Mother and Daddy were Christians, and they always taught us about the Lord Jesus and took us to Sunday School. I didn't have any extra money, and I wanted to get my daddy something for his birthday. All week I could think of only one thing to give him. So I went forward that Sunday morning to make a public statement that I had given my heart to the Lord. I thought that was the greatest gift you could give anyone. It did make my dad happy.

My father had been in sports since he was a little boy. He was born in 1922 in Williamsport, Kentucky, as one of sixteen children. In order to get extra money for lunch, he was very good at marbles. He was the champ. He would beat everyone and win a nickel so that he could buy extra milk. One tends to be very competitive with a large family. My dad went on to hold the Kentucky State Basketball scoring record in 1941 and was drafted by the Pittsburgh Pirates in baseball. At the same time the Pirates drafted him, so did the Army.

It was my father's love for sports that got me into tennis. I started playing tennis at age thirteen on the tennis courts behind the Pikeville College Gymnasium in Pikeville, Kentucky. The courts were located right beside my house. My father was athletic director, basketball coach, and baseball coach at the college. Because Daddy loved sports so much, I reasoned that if I were good at sports I could be with him even more. I was very competitive, and I worked hard. I started playing with the college students. They knew us all: my sisters, Paula and Ruthie, and me. Daddy lent me a tennis racket from the college. It was a wooden Wilson with which I played my heart out.

I began beating the college students because I had a goal in mind. They were just playing for fun or taking a class that my father was teaching. After about six months I could beat almost all of his students, so he would use me as an example. That was really something special for a thirteen-year-old back in the sixties. It also meant that I was able to be with my daddy more, which was a dream come true.

In the summer of 1962, I started playing tennis with a young man named Kenneth Warren Huffman. This is who the love story is about. He had just graduated from high school, and I had just graduated from the eighth grade. Kenny lived a block away from my house. I used to pass by him when he was washing his car, but he would never speak. He didn't know that I existed until we started hitting tennis. We began to realize we had a lot in common. We were both born in September, and we both loved sports. Tennis, basketball, and baseball were our favorites. Tennis became number one.

At first, I was just playing tennis as I did with anyone else. But soon we started meeting three or four times a week to play tennis. Eventually, it was every day that it didn't rain. Kenny was very popular in school. Many of his friends would drive by and visit with him while we were playing. This made me very nervous. I just stayed silent and listened. As we continued to play tennis, things between us began changing. My heart would flutter every time we walked on the court.

We were very competitive. He would hit hard, and I would hit harder. Then we learned to slice the ball and put spin on it. Our serves became much harder. I didn't serve like the young girls do today. My first serve and second serve were equally hard, and so were Kenny's. Of course, there wasn't any money on the line, but I don't remember many double faults. We just knew we would get it in.

After about two months, we were flirting around with each other. We would talk about what it was like dating people each other's age. Our tennis matches were heating up. Sometimes our tennis score might have been love–30, but our love for one another, even at a young age, was growing. I will never forget the time one of us hit a tennis ball over the eight-foot fence, and it rolled down the hill. We both had to look for it. Balls were scarce then. While we searched, Kenny told me that dating someone his age was not like dating someone my age; it was far more serious. My heart was thumping that afternoon.

At that time, the boy I liked was Woody Hopkins. We were barely thirteen. A date with Woody meant that we would sit next to each other at the movies. Dating someone Kenny's age meant going someplace in a car, and it also meant asking my parents.

Kenny's birthday and mine were coming up. Mine was on the twelfth, and his was on the thirtieth of September. He waited until I was fourteen to ask me out. I never dreamed my parents would let me go. They always said we could never date until we were sixteen. But my parents knew Kenny's mom and dad, William and Eleanor Huffman, owners of Huffman Drug Store in downtown Pikeville. Kenny picked me up in a black Cadillac. I thought a miracle had happened!

We kept dating and playing tennis. I started teaching young children to play tennis on the Baptist Church tennis courts when I was in high school. I didn't get paid. They wanted to learn, and I loved tennis so much that I didn't mind. So, on Saturday mornings I would teach children. Kenny would help me. The children seemed to enjoy it. It also gave me another opportunity to see Kenny.

Just as Kenny started his freshman year in college, I started my freshman year in high school. His parents bought him a red Pontiac convertible. A fourteen-year-old in 1962 driving around in a Pontiac convertible was truly something! I loved being with Kenny with the top down soaking in the rays. He was being kidded by his friends as "robbing the cradle" for dating someone so young, but thank God it didn't stop him. I used to get so mad at Johnny Sanders, one of his best friends, for teasing him. If you looked in Kenny's billfold, he had pictures of about fifteen girls because everyone just loved him. He was the life of the party. He could have chosen anyone, but he chose me. I was the luckiest girl in the world. It didn't matter to me what his friends said. I was crazy about him. I wasn't going to let him go.

Kenny made the college tennis team his freshman year. When you play players as good or better than you are all the time, you are always going to get better. During the summer, I could win half of the matches that we played. After Kenny started playing on the college team, I might win one out of five matches, if I was lucky. He surely did get better. The whole town knew he was good. Kenny's brother, Steve, was a good player, too. He used to play some really tough tennis and give us both a run for our money. He is still playing tennis today.

Kenny loved playing college tennis. He was so good that he was hard to beat. I played after school with Kenny. We had many love matches. We played hard and had some disagreements on court and off. It seemed like our tennis matches mirrored our real life: fast and furious for a while until I finally grew up. When you are that young, you want to have your cake and eat it too.

I was popular at school, and Kenny would ask me why I had to be in so many activities and clubs. He loved me, and he wanted me for himself. Had I been older I would have understood. The best place for us to be was on the tennis courts. We could take out all our aggressions on the courts.

My best friends in high school were Ann Blackburn, Madge Walters, Vickie Butcher, and Kay McNeil. I told Ann and Madge that I was going to marry Kenny someday. They said, "How do you know that?" I told them, "Because God told me so." Paula, my sister, liked Kenny also, but I told her to forget about it—he was mine! Nobody believed how determined I was about dating and marrying Kenny.

I also had another friend who was a boy. He was a great friend all through high school. His name was Joe Dawahare. I could tell him anything. It seemed easier to talk to a boy, because there was no jealousy and no competition. We could talk over our problems and come away relieved.

It seems that in life there are many lessons to learn. The Lord is the best teacher. Our parents are good teachers, and sports is a good teacher. Sports teaches you discipline and helps you mature. That maturity hopefully will carry you through other avenues of your life. I know it has mine. Without tennis and the experiences I shared in tennis, I wouldn't have turned to the Lord so much, and I wouldn't be the person I am today. I am grateful for all these experiences in tennis and with the Lord and in life.

Kenny and I entered small tournaments in town. There weren't many in such a small town back in the sixties. We always won the doubles. Then came along a protégé named Lee Smith. We started playing with Lee when he was young and brought him along until he became a very good player. Kenny helped him a lot with his tennis. Then Lee started winning, beating both of us sometimes. The first tournament we entered was the Jaycee Open Tennis Tournament held at the Pikeville College Courts on July 21, 1966. Kenny and I both won the tournament. He defeated Lee Lindsey in the men's singles, and I defeated Jean Williamson in the women's singles. The tournament was sponsored by the Pikeville Jaycees to benefit the community. The Pikeville Jaycees sponsored several other tournaments that Kenny won. (Article 1, Picture 1) This article was written up in the *Pike County News* July 21, 1966.

Huffman, Taylor, Butcher
Winners in Jaycee Open

The Jaycee Open Tennis Tournament was held at the Pikeville College Courts on Friday and Saturday of this past week, and there were 15 players in the tourney. Kenny Huffman defeated Lee Lindsey in the Men's Finals 6–2, 6–2. Sue Butcher defeated Jean Williamson 6–0, 6–0 in the Woman's Finals. In the Junior Division, Bill Doug Taylor defeated Bobby Combs 6–3, 6–2. Trophies were awarded in each division.

H .L. Yelverton, tourney director, said that the tournament was a success, and that next year's tourney should be even better. Next year's plans include an invitation to the various Tennis Clubs through-out the state to send players to compete with the Pikeville players. This is another of the many great projects supported by the Pikeville Jaycees to benefit the community. (End Article)

Sue Butcher—Kenny Huffman
Our First Tennis Tournament

Tennis was beginning to pick up in the Pikeville area. The college had just built four new courts, and they were full every day. Kenny caused much enthusiasm for tennis in the 1960s and early '70s. Everyone wanted to beat him.

Another tournament Kenny entered was between July 8 and July 17, 1969. It was the Pikeville Men's Single Tennis

Tournament. The winner of the tournament was, of course, Kenny. The following article (Article 2) was written up in the Pike County News.

Huffman Wins Tennis Crown

The Pikeville Men's Single Tennis Tournament has been completed. The tournament which was scheduled to last from July 8 through July 12 actually lasted from July 8 to July 17. It was a double elimination tournament consisting of 15 players and the enthusiasm shown promises an even larger turnout in the future. At the conclusion of the tournament, a watermelon feast was held and the winner received a plaque with the runners-up receiving cups.

Participating in the tournament were: Tim Adams, Paul Butcher, Chris Chrisman, Butch Crew, Chuck Damron, Joe Dawahare, Hugh B. Hall, John Hancock, John Doug Hayes, Woody Hopkins, Kenny Huffman, Steve Huffman, Steve Lumas and Jim Todd. The winner of the tournament was Kenny Huffman who won the final sets, 6–1, 6–0. The first runner-up was Doug Hayes and the second runner-up Jim Todd.

The singles tournament paved the way for a doubles tournament to be held the third week in August. All persons wishing to participate should contact Sue or Kenny Huffman by August 15. An entry fee of one dollar will be charged to pay for trophies. Both men and women may participate. (End Article)

In my senior year of high school, Kenny's senior year of college, we wanted to get married. We knew we couldn't. Kenny had to finish college and get a job, and I was still a minor. It was a struggle. We just kept playing tennis, tennis, tennis. Every chance we got we played with anyone that was good enough to play. Most of the time we played doubles, so we learned to be good doubles partners. I was a much better singles player. Kenny was good at both.

I tried to fit everything in. My grades were very important to me. I couldn't stand to make a B. Of course, occasionally that would happen, but I studied very hard. I was also a cheerleader, so we always had practices after school. But every day I couldn't wait until Kenny would pick me up after cheerleading practice and bring me home. If time allowed, we would hit the courts and go at it. Then I would go in and study to prepare for the next day. It was one of the most wonderful times of my life.

On the court, we were pretty serious. Off the court, we liked to have a lot of fun during my high school years. Because I was a cheerleader, Kenny came to every basketball and football game. We had a blast. After the game, we would all go out to Jerry's Restaurant and celebrate. This would give us another chance to be together. We used every excuse we could to see each other. I would go with him to the college basketball and baseball games. My father, of course, was still the coach. I loved that.

I remember one occasion when Kenny and I got really brave. It was the only time in my life I ever did anything like this. We got this "great idea" to go to the Jenny Wiley State Park. So, I wrote a fake doctor's excuse and got out of school one afternoon. Kenny and I drove down to the lake in his convertible. It took an hour to get there, but it was worth it. I've never felt such freedom and so much in love. I'll never forget the experience. We felt that this must be what it would be like if we were married.

Kenny's brother, Steve, got married when I was a junior in high school. Everyone kept asking us if we were "next." This thrilled me to pieces. Of course, I wanted to be married even at the age of seventeen, but we both knew I was too young. There were so many more experiences I needed to go through, and we needed more experiences together as a couple.

During my senior year, I was nominated for prom attendant. I wanted to become the queen because when Kenny was in high school he was the prom king, but I didn't win. I was still very proud to have Kenny walk me down the floor as attendant. We were a very handsome couple. We danced until almost midnight with our friends. My parents had always enforced a twelve o'clock curfew. My friends were having parties and breakfasts until morning, but I wasn't allowed to go. That was all right — Kenny didn't want me to go, anyway. We still had a great time.

High school was exciting, but it was difficult to go through. I was dating steady all through high school. I rarely ever went out with my friends. I really enjoyed everyone during the day, because I didn't get to see them much any other time. When you date steady, you have to make a choice. I don't regret the choice I made. The choice was Kenny all the way.

The summer after I graduated, Kenny joined the Army Reserves. He had to go to Fort Knox. That was the first time we were ever away from each other. It was awful. My heart was torn apart; I missed him so much. It made me realize what it was like when soldiers had to go off to war. I don't know how our parents got through the war years. We wrote so many love letters. They were so sweet and loving. I could feel Kenny's love in those letters. I still have them today in a sealed box. I think it was the first time in my life I knew what true love really was. This man really loved me with all of his heart. All this time, from the time I was thirteen, he had been waiting on me to grow up. That's what I call everlasting love.

I still did some crazy things my freshman year of college while Kenny was in the reserves. I was growing up, trying to fit in, be popular, be a cheerleader, and still date Kenny. Trying to fit it all in was puzzling. When it came down to it, I knew where my heart was, and I knew the Lord had told me who my husband was supposed to be.

In 1967, I joined the men's tennis team at Pikeville College. They didn't have a girl's team. My father was athletic director and president of the Eastern Division of the NAIA. He had to call a board meeting and get a special rule passed to let me play. I don't think they believed I would pose a threat to the guys, but I did. I ended up playing #3 singles. I finished with a 500 season. The boys across the net would bomb out when they saw a girl playing. First they would play easy. Then, when they saw that I could play, they would get angry and play as hard as they could. I just laughed inside. That was one of my happiest years in tennis, because I kept getting better and better. The only problem was, it made me so nervous for my daddy to watch me that he had to sneak around corners to watch so I wouldn't see him. I loved and respected him so much that I didn't want to lose. I thought it would hurt him, even though later I realized he was just glad I was doing something I enjoyed.

Kenny came home from boot camp in March, 1967, and we continued dating. In the summer we started talking about getting married. He knew he had to get a job. He had a college degree with a major in physical education and a minor in history. He needed a job immediately, so he went down to The First National Bank (now called the BB&T) and asked for a job as a teller. He got the job and kept it for six years. Further along that summer, we talked more about commitment to one another because I was only eighteen, and he was twenty-two. We both wanted to be sure we were ready for such a serious commitment, especially when you have dated for five years and along the way you have flirted with other people. It was just like making a call in tennis. You want to be sure you call the lines correctly so you don't pay the price for it later. Of course, in life it is a much bigger price. You have peoples' lives at stake. Once we got that settled, Kenny thought it was time to talk to my father. My father thought a lot of Kenny. He already knew our feelings for one another, and he and Mother were happy to give their blessing.

We continued playing tennis all summer long right up to our wedding on August 12, 1967, President Kennedy's birthday. We were so much in love. We thought we had the world in our hands. We each had the blessing of our parents. After our wedding we were going to stay at Mr. and Mrs. Huffman's home until the small brick house at 101 Elm Street became available. It had been rented out and would come available about three weeks after the wedding.

Our wedding was beautiful. I had five bridesmaids and a maid of honor. Paula (my older sister) and Madge, Kay, Vickie, and Ann (my friends) were my bridesmaids; and Ruthie (my younger sister) was my maid of honor. Reverend Curtis Warf married us in the First Baptist Church of Pikeville. Of course, Mother and Mr. and Mrs. Huffman were seated on the front row while my father gave me away. I was being given away by my father, whom I loved so dearly, to the man I loved with my whole heart before God and two hundred people. I was a nervous wreck! At that moment, I just wanted it to be over with so that I could be back on the tennis court, where I knew I could forget it all and just play tennis.

Somehow we made it through the service. I cried when my daddy lifted up the veil and kissed me. I knew I wasn't his little girl any more—I belonged to Kenny now. Lighting the unity candle was so special. I remember shaking as I looked at Kenny. Finally, as Reverend Warf pronounced us husband and wife, Kenny kissed me. We had finally done it! We actually were married after five years of dating and tennis.

It seemed as if each person went out of his way to make the wedding perfect. I remember Velma Childers helped conduct the events of the day. She did a wonderful job. Mr. and Mrs. Huffman gave us a reception at the Pikeville Country Club. It was a very pretty setting. Everyone greeted us so warmly and gave us more gifts than I could have ever imagined. But I was young and nervous. I was glad when it was finally all over. I just wanted to get down the road with Kenny. Finally, several hours later, we left in a green Ford Thunderbird for the Smoky Mountains.

We stayed in Gatlinburg, Tennessee, in a Holiday Inn by a lovely stream. We stayed two days, walking by the shops, doing some shopping and sightseeing, and eating at some of the best restaurants. We thanked God for one another and that we had decided to get married. Then we went on to Fort Lauderdale, Florida, for the rest of the two weeks. I had always wanted to see the ocean. This was the first time and, oh—what a thrill! I was like a little kid. Everything on my honeymoon was new and exhilarating, like a breath of fresh air. Just walking in the sand was a thrill. We brought back gifts made of seashells and special things from Florida. Every night we went out to a different fish restaurant to eat because I loved all types of seafood. During the day we spent most of the time on the beach and in the ocean. The whole trip was glorious. Prior to this, I had only been out of the state of Kentucky two times in my life.

I started my sophomore year of college, and Kenny continued working at the First National Bank. We continued to play tennis, except now the tables had turned. I was getting better on the court because Kenny had been away from the game for about six months, but he was catching up fast. Eventually we were about even. He would win, and then I would win. We were a very competitive duo.

That spring I played my second year on the men's tennis team. This time we had a woman coach, which made it easier for me to travel. It was getting harder to play against the guys. They were getting more used to me, but I still had the same results. I ended with a good season and played the same position. I had to get in better shape. I had weighed about 130 pounds and was five feet six inches tall and was very large-boned. That was not a large size back in 1968. What I didn't know was that I was two months pregnant. I had been married eight months and had put on ten pounds. Unknowingly, I was playing tennis and water skiing while pregnant.

Those were the days. We would go to church Sunday morning, have the boat packed up, and leave for the lake right after the church meeting. Kenny's best friend, Johnny Sanders, and his wife, Beverly, would go to the lake with us. We had a blast. One day Kenny was skiing and ran over a copperhead. That scared me to death. (I was always nervous about getting back in the water after that.) When we came back from the lake, we would play tennis. Isn't youth grand! I'll never forget how much Kenny wanted that boat. One day he decided he couldn't wait any longer. He called the gentleman up who had offered us the boat for a certain price and said we wanted the boat. The very next day we had it. It was my favorite color—blue.

I played tennis for five months into the pregnancy. That was unheard of, but my doctor said it was OK. I loved it. I didn't want to stop playing, but we felt it was best for the baby. When I had to lay my racket down, part of me was missing. I've always missed tennis over the years whenever I haven't been able to play, but I still love the game.

I had little Kenny December 20, 1968. We all thought he was the greatest thing on earth. When you're young, your first child is "everything" to you. My daddy went all over town telling everyone I was giving him a boy. I think I would have felt guilty if my first child had been a girl, because I never wanted to disappoint my father. Of course, he would have been happy no matter what the baby was as long as it was healthy.

My baby boy was named Kenneth Warren Huffman II. He weighed six pounds one ounce and was perfectly healthy. Granddad Butcher and Granddad Huffman got their wish. Granny Butcher and Granny Huffman were thrilled. Of course, my mother knew that with the baby being a boy, my dad would spend all of his time with him. Granny Huffman knew that since Granddad Huffman worked all day, she would have more time with the baby. So, that is what happened. Everyone loved him. Kenny and I were thrilled that he was a boy, but we were happier still that he was healthy. Kenny sort of wanted a girl so he could call her Missy. His wish came true later on.

I had Kenny on Christmas break and went back to college as soon as school started. I never missed a day. My mother taught me to finish what I started. She also taught me to do my best at everything I ever did, so… I had about a 3.7

grade point average in college. I thought that would make her happy.

Kenny and I kept playing tennis. The grandparents would keep Little Kenny while we played tennis. Kenny was able to play more than I could now because of the baby, and, of course, he was better. I didn't like that very much. I tried very much not to show it. Steve Huffman and Lee Smith were beating me, too. I started working harder, but it was difficult with a baby. Men don't always understand that when you have a baby, and you are athletic, you still want to play sports. I used to ask my dad why it was like that, but he said that was just the way men were. So I accepted it.

We played tennis every chance we could. Many times Kenny played with the guys. There weren't any women playing competitive tennis who were in our town at that time except Jean Williamson. She was good, but we never seemed to hook up. I had to play men. I played Kenny most of the time. Sometimes I played Steve Huffman or Lee Smith. Daddy would volunteer to play when he had the time. Most of the time, I was playing with my little boy. I adored him. He was a dream come true. At that time in my life, I had three men who seemed to love me so much. I was very blessed.

Kenny was now going to church with me at the First Baptist Church where we were married. My father was his

Sunday school teacher. Kenny and I both needed to grow in the Lord in order for our marriage to grow. We loved each other so much, but no marriage is perfect. It's just like tennis. You can stay at love only for so long—eventually things have to change, or the game ends. Ask Pete Sampras or Andre Agassi, my two favorite players.

Pete Sampras, in my opinion, is the best tennis player that ever lived. I have watched and played tennis since I was thirteen, since John McEnroe and Jimmy Connors. I have been to tennis camps with Rod Laver and Roy Emerson, whom I respect greatly. I'm sure they don't remember me. I'm unknown. I've watched Bjorn Borg, Arthur Ash, Mats Wilander, Edberg, Ivan Lendl, Boris Becker, Jim Courier, and Michael Chang. I've seen videos of the older greats and tournaments of the newest greats such as Roger Federer and Rafael Nadal. All of these were great, but no one has been aggressive consistently or had that winning spirit as much as Pete Sampras had, and none of them have won fourteen Grand Slams. Besides, he looks like and has the mannerisms of my youngest son, Brad. Even if Federer wins fourteen Grand Slams, this is a different era. It is Sampras all the way.

Andre Agassi has the best longevity of any tennis player ever. Not only that, but he has won eight Grand Slams and has a heart of gold. He has done more for the tennis world and a lot for the education of humanity by starting the Andre Agassi Preparatory Academy. He also has great human character. He is married to the world's greatest female player, and that doesn't hurt things much. I would love for these two tennis players to come to Pikeville and give a tennis exhibition before one of our tournaments. This would be a real boost.

Kenny and I continued with married life and tennis. Kenny loved the game. He would play with everyone every chance he got. We usually worked our problems out on the courts and with the Lord. We were both pretty strong-willed, except I was stronger-willed and younger. I had a long way to go and a lot of growing up to do. Thank God my love for Kenny and little Kenny were stronger than my will. They were both wonderful.

Christmas was a time in our lives that we enjoyed every year. Every year I would get so excited waiting to see what Kenny would get me. This particular year (1968) was a little unusual. I had just delivered little Kenny five days before, and I was still very sick. But when I opened the big present, all I could do was smile. I will never forget the gift. It was a big family Bible. I will always treasure the Bible he gave me.

Kenny loved his mom and dad very much. He was closer to his mom than his dad. It was that mother and son thing. Boys always seem to be closer to their moms. We always called his mom "Mother Superior" because she was always right. We always did everything she said. Kenny and I had a lot of love and respect for her. I already had a wonderful mother. It was so sweet to love my mother-in-law, also. She loved us all so much. She loved little Kenny with all her heart. She would have kept him all day if she could have, but she had to help Granddad Huffman at the pharmacy. We would have played more tennis, too. Of course, Kenny had to work at the bank. I had to continue college, Mother had to teach, and Daddy had to coach. I got a part-time baby-sitter and worked my schedule out so I didn't have to be away more than four hours. Life was great. We were so much in love.

I like the word "love" used in life, in tennis, and with the Lord. It has a different meaning in all three areas. It is amazing how the game of tennis can have such an impact on someone's life. I really never knew how much it had on mine until I watched Pete Sampras at the US Open win his fourteenth Grand Slam in 2001 and Andre Agassi at the US Open in 2006.

I had been wanting to write my tennis love story for ten years. First, I had to wait until I knew that it wouldn't offend my present husband, Brad. Then, I had to make sure my children and family would accept it. After that, I had to pray and ask the Lord to help me. My husband read part of it and said it was the best love story he had ever read. He encouraged me to please finish it, so I had the freedom to continue. Still, it required soul-searching, and many times I was brought to tears.

Kenny and I had two more loves: basketball and baseball. If Kenny wasn't on the tennis courts, you would probably find him playing basketball in the gym. My dad coached the varsity team at Pikeville College, and Kenny helped coach the freshman team one year. This is the team Kenny coached with Sherman Combs. Daddy is on the right side of the picture. (Picture 2)

Kenny and Sherman Combs on left
Coach Butcher on the right

Picture 3 is a picture of Kenny and his mother, Eleanor Huffman, at one of the Pikeville College ball games

Kenny and Granny Huffman

Kenny was also Daddy's trainer for a couple of years when he was in college. He really loved my father. Daddy wasn't a difficult person to love. Most everyone loved and respected my father. No wonder Mother loved him so much and misses him so much today. Daddy died in February, 1998. It was very difficult for all of us, especially Mother.

Kenny and I often went to the Pikeville College games. When we could, we traveled to the Kentucky Wildcat games in Lexington. Back then, that was the biggest highlight there was. And it still is. I'm a Kentucky Wildcat fan through and through. I haven't been to a game since the seventies. I would love to sit on the front row and see a game, but today I would probably have to have a special chair. When we used to go to the games, it didn't matter where we sat. We just had a great time. We always met some friends and cheered our team on to victory. After the game, we had to drive three and a half hours to get home, but it was worth it.

Kentucky didn't have a pro baseball team, so the closest team to us was the Cincinnati Reds. We loved the Reds. Kenny and I went a couple of times. It was a blast. We would always root for Johnny Bench and Pete Rose. Today, since we live in Atlanta, our whole family loves the Braves. Out of ten grandchildren, I have six playing baseball or softball. It was difficult to make it to all of their games, even though I tried really hard. I still missed a lot of games. I had about fifty games in all, and I made it to about thirty-two.

Isn't life strange, yet wonderful, and awful, yet joyful—all at the same time? You can find what you want out of life. It is according to what you put into it and whom you love and trust. I guess that from the time I met Kenny, my life changed for the better. He was my Prince Charming. No one in eighth grade summer school believed me when I told them I was going to date Kenny Huffman, a guy getting ready to start college. But, I knew I was. I could feel the vibes. The more we played tennis, the more I knew it. My mind was made up, and nobody was going to change it. I knew Kenny felt the same way that I did, even though I was very young.

I had to put my racket up for a few months my senior year of college. I was expecting again. I had Little Kenny at the age of twenty. I was so thrilled not to be a teenage mom. Now at twenty-two I was pregnant again. In the seventies, you didn't have an ultrasound to see what sex your child was going to be. Kenny really wanted a girl. He wanted to name her Susan Melissa. The 'Susan' was after me.

On spring break from college, we had Missy. Oh, what a joy! She weighed seven pounds and eight ounces, and had blue eyes and blond hair. Everyone was so happy. Now Mother was rejoicing. She had her baby girl. Missy was a delight to her father. When she was a baby, he would sit and hold her or just play with her. Even when she was barely one year old, he would read books to her or take her for a stroll. He loved to spend time with her.

We were very happy. We had each other, Kenny II, and Missy—and we still got to play tennis on the evenings and weekends. Granny and Granddad Huffman were so happy. There had not been any girls born in the Huffman family. Missy was the first. She was our little princess. I'll never forget how much Granddad Huffman loved her. He used to carry her around with her pigtails flopping back and forth. Every time we went to their house, he would sit Missy on his lap and would read to her a new book he had bought.

Kenny would take little Kenny to the gym and run the lines or play basketball during the winter when he was two and three. In the summer, Kenny, Daddy, and I would play baseball with him. We nicknamed him "Kenny Boy" when he was just a baby, and it stuck with him as long as we lived in Pikeville. Kenny Boy loved playing baseball. It eventually became his favorite sport. Later on, when Kenny Boy was three and four, Kenny would hit a little tennis with him. Kenny Boy seemed to love to play sports with his dad and granddad. With Missy being so small, we played around the house with her or took her for walks. Lots of times we showed her off to other people. She had a beautiful smile and long, curly blond hair.

The grandparents added a lot, too. Mother would keep Missy while we played tennis. Mother adored her; the feeling was mutual. I also watched how Daddy and Granny and Granddad Huffman played with her. Daddy used to get down on the floor and let her ride on his back like a horse. She was a barrel of laughs. The children always brightened up any room they were in. Our world was pretty wonderful: Kenny, myself, Kenny Boy, Missy, Mother, Daddy, Granny and Granddad Huffman, tennis, and the Lord. My sisters were also part of our lives. Paula had just had a baby girl named Michelle. Ruthie had a baby girl named Rachel, and Ruthie always came and helped baby-sit for me so I could clean house or something. It was a family affair.

Kenny and I played tennis in the spring and summer and went to basketball games in the winter. We also went to many of my dad's baseball games at Pikeville College. We took Kenny Boy and Missy everywhere we went except when we went to play tennis. I could never focus on tennis with my children there. Tennis and golf are a lot alike. They require a lot of concentration. You can't have many distractions around. The ball is too small. If you take your eyes off the ball, you lose your focus.

Basketball was Kenny's second favorite sport. If he wasn't playing tennis he would go to the gym and find a game of basketball when he had spare time. We were fortunate because the tennis courts were practically across the street from our house, and the college gym was on the same block. We walked to both of them. We felt like they were ours. We were both very active through the week with work, school, sports, and our two children.

Our favorite vacation was going to Cincinnati to watch Jimmy Connors and John McEnroe play tennis. We only had Kenny Boy at the time, so we threw in the Cincinnati Zoo. It was so much fun watching our little boy try to make all those animal noises and go crazy over every animal. The tournament was the first professional tennis tournament we had ever seen. It fulfilled all of our expectations. It made both of us want to come home and work on our game. I knew for myself, it would be very difficult with my baby boy and school. Still, I played every chance I could get, squeezing it in between going to church, family functions, and basketball. Kenny, of course, played more. I'm so glad he did.

I graduated from college in 1970 and decided to start my master's degree as soon as I could. I always wanted to further my education. In the spring 1971, I was told I had to take nine hours at another university in order to begin my degree. I could not bear to leave Kenny, so he took a short leave of absence from the First National Bank.

We went to Morehead State University and started our master's degrees in physical education, health, and recreation. We took the same classes together. We left our comfortable little home and rented a trailer for the summer just to get our nine hours. The rest we could get back home. At least this was a start. We both figured that we were young, healthy, and smart. Since we were in the same field of education, we could help each other. Why not do it now together while we had the opportunity?

The classes were not hard for me, but Kenny seemed to have a hard time concentrating. Sometimes I would look over at him, and his face would be grimacing. He would hold his side like something was hurting him. I didn't say anything for a long time. Then, when I would ask him what was wrong, he would say, "Nothing." He was just thinking about something. I learned later what was wrong.

That summer was difficult for both of us: studying, caring for the children, attending classes, and caring for things at home. Kenny was still working out and trying to play tennis. I never imagined anything could be wrong with Kenny's physical health. He was supposed to be invincible. We were young. We didn't think our health would ever fail us. It is not supposed to. We were supposed to get to live to be eighty-five or so. Of course, we didn't think about the future. We just knew that we were in love, and we wanted our lives to go on together. We wanted to watch our children grow up and mature, play sports, learn to love the Lord, and get married.

It was far from our minds that we would ever have a life-threatening illness.

That summer, when we came back from school, Kenny went back to work at the bank, and life was beginning to be normal again. The bank offered him the office of vice president. He was considering it until he went to the doctor. Dr. Jones told us there was something wrong that needed further examination. He wanted us to leave for the Mayo Clinic, in Rochester, Minnesota, for tests. I had no idea what was wrong. I certainly did not even dream of cancer.

There was a small knot on Kenny's neck. That was why I wanted him to go to the doctor in the first place—not for any other reason. It turned out that the knot didn't have anything to do with it. My mother kept telling me he looked pale or yellow in his skin color, but I didn't want to believe her. She said this for about two weeks. I just wouldn't believe anything could be wrong with Kenny because I loved him so much. I wasn't going to accept it until I had no choice.

We had never left our children for more than a day. This time we had to pack our bags and leave our babies for an unknown amount of time. I thought it would be for just a couple of days to run some tests. It turned out to be one month. I never dreamed what was coming. I thank God we don't know the future. One day at a time is all I can handle. He promises us that His grace is sufficient.

We left Missy with Mother and Daddy. Mother was a school teacher. She took off work the entire time to keep Missy while we were gone. We didn't worry. She was in great hands. Kenny Boy stayed with Granny and Granddad Huffman. We knew he was being loved every day, so we had no worries.

When we arrived at Mayo Clinic, the doctors had arranged for a variety of examinations on the first day. The next morning, we went to the main doctor to get the results. The doctor's answer was devastating to both of us. He said Kenny had colon cancer, and it had spread to the liver. He put it to us straight. He said it was incurable. There also were some spots on his lungs. *How could this be?* He was only twenty-eight years old. We had two children. My life without Kenny flashed before me, and I broke down and sobbed. Finally, the doctor told us they were going to operate to take a large piece of cancer from Kenny's colon. Then they were going to use some cancer drugs to try to reduce the growth and spreading of the cancer. We were at the best hospital we knew, and this was the best they could do for Kenny.

I know Kenny was heartbroken for both of us, yet he was so strong. He kept telling me that maybe they would get it all and find a cure. Maybe the medicine would work. Most of that night we were pretty silent. We didn't know what to think or say. We talked about it over the next day or two. I know we were in shock. I think I was just too young to handle it. I was twenty-four. If I hadn't loved him so much, it might have been easier, but I don't know if it is ever easier. Today, I have a close friend who just lost her husband to cancer. She and Johnny remind me so much of Kenny and me. It is never easy, no matter what age you are.

By Friday, Kenny was being operated on. Granny and Granddad Huffman and Steve came up to Mayo Clinic to be with us. They left Kenny Boy with Daddy for the weekend. The doctor took out a large piece of cancer that looked like a five-pound roast. It was awful. I remember Granny Huffman, Steve, and I being in the same room talking to the doctor while Kenny was in recovery. The doctor told us the cancer was too far along. He gave him nine months to live. I went to pieces. Granny Huffman tried to console me. It was very hard. I had to collect myself because I had to go talk to Kenny next.

After a while I managed to calm down. I went to the recovery room. There was my sweet husband lying there. I loved him so much I could hardly bear it. We talked for a while about the children, and then he asked me, "Honey, how long do I have, two years?" I didn't have the heart to say anything else. I knew he would make every minute count. To Kenny, life was worth living for. He loved every minute of it. It was filled with joy, family, work, and sports, and he knew his Savior. He wasn't ready to spend the rest of his life in bed. He would make the most of it until he couldn't anymore.

He stayed in the hospital for a week or so, and then we traveled back and forth from the hotel for cancer treatments. We were in Rochester for about a month. When we returned, Kenny brought medicine with him to take at home. We would have to fly back to Mayo Clinic one week every month for about the next eight or nine months. After about the fifth month, they used Kenny as an experimental patient, because nothing was working as well as we had hoped.

Kenny definitely did not come home and give up. He went back to work for four hours a day at the bank. When his hair came out, he wore a toupee. He made a joke of it. That is how he handled things. He was always the life of the party. The toupee cracked everybody up the first day. Then all of his co-workers got used to it. The bank allowed him to work as many hours as he could. He played some tennis. We would hit around, not hard and serious, but we were still playing tennis. Kenny would hit around with Kenny Boy, too. He would also take Kenny Boy to the gym and run the lines with him and shoot some basketball. It hurt to watch him, but I wouldn't say anything. I knew he wanted to be with his son as long as he could.

Kenny and I tried to live as normally as possible. He always woke up, got dressed, and walked to work as long as he was able. After work, he would come home and rest for a while, then play with the children. We continued going to the ball games, and it meant a lot when Kenny's friends would come by to visit. It took his mind off the cancer. They always got him laughing over all the things they got away with when they were young.

Kenny had so many friends from high school. Three friends in particular always stayed in touch: Johnny Sanders, John Doug Hays, and Robert Carter. These friends had been through a lot together, good and bad. They could tell some big tales, many of which I didn't want to hear. Many times they would tell me stories about some of their high school or college trips just to get me jealous, and then they would start laughing. I look back on it, and am so thankful for those guys.

When Kenny would rest, he would read the Bible. He read many chapters from many books. One book in particular he kept reading over and over again was the book of Job. He wanted to be sure he understood every bit of it. At first he was very perplexed, but after reading it for about the fourth or fifth time, a great peace came over him. I believe he finally understood that God just wanted to gain more of Job. Job had everything, and he needed to think more about God so he could be an expression of God, a living testimony. I know Kenny was a testimony to me, especially in the fact that he read his Bible every day and in the way he lived. He had faith right up to the end. Many other people told me the same thing.

As the days went on, one week out of the month we still had to go to Mayo Clinic. That became our schedule. The trip became more difficult until we finally stopped. It was wearing Kenny down. His body was becoming more fragile and weak. Part of Kenny's schedule was taking rides with Johnny Sanders. Johnny would take Kenny and Kenny Boy for a ride all around Pikeville about four times a week just to get him out of the house. They went to many different sites. If he felt too bad, they wouldn't go. Johnny was very considerate of Kenny. Kenny Boy would always go with them.

Kenny and I would watch television at night after we put the kids to bed, if he felt well enough and if time allowed. One night he made me watch the movie, *Love Story*. I cried my eyes out. I didn't want to finish watching it, but he said I had to, so I did. It was about a girl dying of cancer. I prayed that night for the Lord to give me the strength to get through this, because all my strength was gone. I was running on fumes.

We still attended church services every Sunday morning. It was getting harder for Kenny to sit though the meetings because the pain continued to get worse, and he had lost a lot of weight. One Sunday he sat on the back row with my daddy while my sister Paula and I sang a duet. The song was "I Believe in Miracles." There weren't many dry eyes in the church building. I still believed he would be healed, that somehow he would get well. He stayed for about an hour, and then we had to leave so that he could go home and rest.

During those eleven months, many things changed between us and in many people's lives. We saw how fragile life really can be and how we have to live one day at a time. We had to put our trust in the Lord. We also realized we can't take anything for granted, especially our health. It was during these times that our family became very special to us. We were so fortunate to have each other, the children, and our parents. Kenny's parents had treated me like a daughter, and my parents had treated Kenny like a son.

The whole community had been praying for us. People would walk down the street and tell me they were praying for us. This was a different world I was living in. Beverly Sanders told me her whole prayer life changed. She said she learned that, "God in His time is always right."

Kenny worked half days up until two weeks before he died. The bank had been very understanding toward him. Then he came home and never went back. His body was worn out from fighting all the cancer. We had tried everything. Every medication we knew of did not work. It was time to rest a while. I was going to care for him by myself at home. I knew Kenny's mother would help me. I would not put him in the hospital, not until the last night.

Kenny bought me a card and wrote in it that he would like to be with the Lord, but he would stay here as long as he could because of me. I had another crying spell. I cried a lot those days, but I did it most of the time when he wasn't looking. I tried to be brave around him and the children. I wonder how in the world I raised my children during that time. I am so thankful that I had Kenny and Missy. They helped keep me busy and keep my mind off the cancer. God knew I needed those children.

Finally, the night before he died, he fell out of bed. I had to call for help. Granny Huffman was with me. I also called Johnny Sanders and John Doug Hayes to come and help me. When they arrived, they went upstairs and gave Kenny a sponge bath so we could get him ready to go to the hospital.

In my mind I knew it was time, but in my heart, I wasn't ready to let go. The ambulance finally arrived, and we all left to go to the Methodist Hospital.

That night in the hospital room, Kenny went into a coma and remained in one for many hours. Granny and Granddad Huffman and I were there with him. The nurses and doctor kept checking on him to see how he was doing. They were checking to see if his bodily functions were still operating and if he was still alive. I finally lay down on a cot in the room and rested for a few hours for the first time in months. I prayed for the Lord to take him if He wasn't going to heal him. I didn't want him to suffer any longer. He had suffered long enough. It was time for my wonderful husband to go on and be with the Lord. I hoped that some day I could explain what a great husband he had been to me and what a great dad he had been to the kids.

Soon Granny Huffman told me it was time. Kenny was about to go. So I went close to his bed and hugged him and told him I loved him. Then tears came out the sides of his eyes. I know he heard me. Then he died. It seemed like my world came to an end. My high school sweetheart, my best friend, my husband, my lover, the father of my children, my tennis partner, and my future was gone. *What do I do now? Where do I go from here?* Only God could answer these questions.

I remember Granny Huffman telling me it was time to go home now. I said that I didn't have a home to go to.

I think I was mildly sedated for a couple of days. I went to the funeral home for two days and greeted all the people that came. I never dreamed so many people knew and loved Kenny so much. They all had such wonderful things to say about him and how he had been such a good testimony to them. This made me very happy. I'll never forget Gene Davis. He worked at the bank with Kenny. They were good friends and were very close. He said some very kind words to me as he always did. Of course, we wouldn't have been able to make it without Steve, Kenny's brother. He was such a great help to me and his mother. Mother and Daddy were a big help. They would keep the children so I could take care of all the matters. This is not something you want to go through when you are young. But, if you know your loved one is saved, then it eases the pain.

Granny and Granddad Huffman were with me every step of the way. With every decision I made, they helped me; otherwise I couldn't have done it. They are wonderful in-laws.

We buried Kenny at the Johnson Memorial Cemetery in Pikeville, Kentucky, with a double tombstone. On the tombstone is engraved, "Not my will, but Thine be done."

This is what I have always wanted to live by. I don't regret putting it there. Also engraved on the tombstone is, "This marriage was made in heaven." I have it decorated every year.

It has now been thirty-five years since Kenny died. I still think about him a lot, and they are such sweet memories. Now I can tell my children and my second husband all the fun and crazy things we did, and we laugh about it.

After the funeral, we all had to try to live our lives. It wasn't easy. I still wanted to play tennis. I tried to play with almost anybody, but it wasn't the same. It was hard finding a partner. Many times, Steve or Daddy would play with me, but I always felt empty. Of course, Mother had fun babysitting Missy. She loved playing with her and strolling around with her. Daddy spent many evenings at my house keeping me company, talking about basketball and such. He was trying to take my mind off Kenny so I wouldn't cry myself to sleep, as I did every night. Most nights, I would read the Bible until I fell to sleep or cried myself to sleep for a long time. You think you are strong until death knocks at your door and shakes you. At this point, my daddy became my best friend again. He kept me going for a long time. He reminded me that I had two good reasons to live—Kenny and Missy. They were two precious gifts Kenny had left me, and I needed to show them a lot of love. I also needed to be strong for the Lord.

That first year was the hardest year of my life. I felt completely lost. I stayed mostly around my family. Instead of having a partner to go places with, I was by myself. When I went to church meetings or ball games or visited friends, it felt odd. Sometimes I didn't even know what to say because all of my friends were also Kenny's. I felt his presence everywhere, especially on the tennis courts. The tears seemed to never end.

It was always wonderful to have my children with me. They kept me busy and active, and they made me laugh. It was good to tell them about their dad so they could remember him when they get older. We always went over to the grandparents' houses during the week and on the weekends. I always wanted them to be close to their grandparents.

There were several articles written in the local newspaper and one in the *Kentucky Banker* about Kenny that really blessed me. The one written in the *Pike County News* by Bob Tarbeck, the local sports writer, was very expressive and explained Kenny's courage. I really liked this one. (Article 3, written in 1973)

Sport Notes and Tribute
BY: BOB TARBECK

The entire area, a wide area, mourns the recent passing of Kenny Huffman. It was once said to me that one would give all of his yesterdays for one more tomorrow. Kenny's yesterdays were filled with goodness and the tomorrow's will be better one's for those of us who knew him. The definition of the word courage was spelled KENNY HUFFMAN. He faced life with courage and faced death as he faced life, with courage, an even greater courage. He will not be on the sports scene but he'll not be forgotten. (End Article 3)

In October, 1973 an article in the *Kentucky Banker* gave respect and honor to Kenny. (Article 4)

IN MEMORIAM
Kenneth W. Huffman

WHEREAS God in his infinite wisdom has called from our midst KENNETH W. HUFFMAN, BE IT RESOLVED that The First National Bank of Pikeville will miss him from our ranks. He faithfully served this bank as Assistant Cashier since June 1967.

BE IT RESOLVED that this institution was fortunate to have had such a loyal employee, and WHEREAS the loss to his family was greater, his service and devotion to this institution will be missed.

The Secretary of the Board was instructed to see that a copy of this Resolution was made a part of the minutes of this meeting and that said Resolution be published in the Pike County News, Williamson Daily News and the Kentucky Banker.

BOARD OF DIRECTORS
FIRST NATIONAL BANK OF PIKEVILLE
John E. Coleman, Secretary

(End of Article)

A dear friend of Kenny's wrote a poem about him and had it published in the newspaper. Trimble Maynard expressed how much everybody loved Kenny. (Article 5)

Kenny

Come all you kind people
And listen while I tell
The story of Dear Kenny
The one we loved so well
He was kind to everybody
Helped in every way he could
And oh! How we miss him
He was so good, so good.

Now to his wife and children
I know your hearts are sad
For you will miss a loving husband
And a dear kind dad.
TRIMBLE MAYNARD

(End Article)

Weeks after Kenny died, I kept going through his personal items, and I found many special things he had in his billfold. He also had some special verses underlined in his Bible. This really, really thrilled me. It helped me to understand him better. One of the things was a card with "The Lord Is My Shepherd—Psalms 23" imprinted on it. It had all six verses on it. He carried it in his billfold everywhere he went. He was at the point in his life where the Lord was truly his Shepherd. Kenny really didn't want anything but to be with the Lord. I also found these verses underlined in his Bible: I Peter 1:4–6. "And God, in His mighty power, will make sure that you get there safely to receive it, because you are trusting Him. It will be yours in that coming last day for all to see. So be truly glad! There is wonderful joy ahead, even though the going is rough for a while down here." These verses have been such an encouragement to me through all these years. Just to know what my loving husband was looking forward to – a mighty hope.

Going through my husband's things after he died was very difficult, but I had so many precious memories. Most of the time I cried a lot while I went through them, but I was so blessed to read all these wonderful things. It was all the pictures that tore me up, as well as the trophies that we had won while playing tennis together. I could hardly stand it. I was so glad I had my family and the Lord. I also remembered all the precious gifts Kenny bought me.

One thing I loved to get was jewelry. Kenny always picked things out by himself. So when he gave me something, I knew it came from his heart. I was never disappointed in anything he ever bought me because every item was beautiful, especially the scarab bracelet. That was one of my favorites. I had wanted a scarab bracelet for years, and finally Kenny bought me one during my senior year of high school. I loved that bracelet. I wore it everywhere. I hardly ever took it off.

One day at school, I was getting ready to go out to play softball in physical education. For some reason I didn't want to wear my bracelet. I was afraid I would damage it in some way, so I left it in the gym. When I came back to get it, it was gone. My heart was broken. I couldn't believe it. I searched everywhere for it. All my friends helped me. We searched for days. We asked everyone. It never reappeared.

Another favorite of the gifts Kenny gave me was an elegant silver watch. It was so dainty; I treasured it. I only took it off to wash my hands or to shower. I wore it for years. Kenny seemed to always know what I liked. He had great taste.

My third favorite gift was a silver locket that was given to me the last year that Kenny was alive. This locket meant the world to me, because of what was written inside. Kenny had bought me a birthday card that had a lovely phrase which read, "You alone will always be the one who means the world to me." He took the locket to the jewelry store and had the phrase printed inside the locket. That is the most meaningful gift Kenny ever gave to me. I still have it today as a keepsake. I have wonderful memories.

I decided, several months after Kenny died, to do something in Kenny's memory. I contacted the college and talked to Bill Higginbotham, Vice President of Public Relations. We discussed starting a scholarship in Kenny's memory. I also asked if the college would rename the tennis courts after him. The Kenneth Warren Huffman Memorial Scholarship was started in 1973 at Pikeville College. It was to help young people in the sport of tennis. (Article 6, Sept.27, 1973)

SCHOLARSHIP STARTED — Susie Huffman, wife of the late Kenneth W. Huffman, has given Pikeville College President Robert S. Cope, $2,000 to inaugurate a tennis endowment scholarship. Dr. Cope said the money would be used for a perpetual scholarship in the name of Kenneth W. Huffman

Memorial Scholarship. Dr. Cope has announced the tennis courts on the college's lower campus will be renamed in honor of Huffman who was instrumental in starting many young people in the area in tennis. Huffman was employed by the First National Bank of Pikeville at the time of his death. He was the son of Mr. and Mrs. William Milton Huffman of Pikeville and the son-in-law of Pikeville College athletic director, Paul Butcher. (End Article)

This scholarship fund turned out to be very important to the sport of tennis at the college. It helped the college move up the ranks in tennis, and it helped many local players. One of the hometown players it helped was Lee Smith, of whom both Kenny and I thought very highly.

That year, we started a tournament in Pikeville and played it on the courts that were named after Kenny. It was called "The Kenneth Warren Huffman Memorial Tennis Tournament." It was played in late September. Sports Enterprise and Pikeville College sponsored it, and the First National Bank sponsored the trophies. Lee Smith won the tournament. (Article 7, Picture 4)

The first annual Kenneth W. Huffman Tennis Tournament was held this past weekend at the Pikeville College Tennis Courts. The tournament was in memory of one of Pikeville's best tennis players who recently passed away. The tournament was jointly sponsored by Sports-Enterprise of Pikeville and Pikeville College. The winner of the tournament was Lee Smith, a 16-year old high school student from Pikeville. He defeated Pikeville College basketball player George Preece 6–2, 6–1 in the final match. Preece had defeated Steve Huffman in the semifinal round 6–0, 6–0 and Smith had defeated Sue Huffman 6–3, 6–1. (End Article)

PIKE COUNTY NEWS, PIKEVILLE, KY.

Lee Smith Wins
Memorial Tennis Tournament

SMITH
(Left)

PREECE
(Right)

Lee Smith—George Preece

The fund for the tournament and the turnout had been favorable. Everyone enjoyed it. I tried my best, but I still could not beat Lee Smith. All of the funds went toward the scholarship fund to recruit tennis players for the college. Tennis was growing in the area, and the tournament really helped. The *Pike County News* publicized all of the tournaments.

The second annual Kenneth Warren Huffman Memorial Tennis Tournament was held June 17–22, 1974, on the same courts. It was still sponsored by Sports-Enterprise and Pikeville College with the First National Bank sponsoring the trophies. This time, Lee Smith won the singles title again, but I lucked out and won the doubles with Lee. We played very well together. We had to play four rounds before we finally won. I was happy to win my husband's tournament, but I had to hold back the tears during the pictures. (Article 8)

> *The second annual Kenneth W. Huffman Memorial Tennis Tournament was held June 17–22 at the Kenneth W. Huffman Memorial Tennis Courts located on the Pikeville College lower campus.*
>
> *The tournament was in memory of one of Pikeville's best tennis players. It was sponsored by Pikeville College and Sports-Enterprise of Pikeville.*
>
> *The doubles trophies were sponsored by the First National Bank of Pikeville, and the singles trophies were sponsored by Marley's Barber Shop and Sports-Enterprise.*

Gene Davis, from the First National Bank was present to present the trophies to the winners and runners up of the Doubles Title.

The winner of the Singles Title was Lee Smith, a 17 year-old high school student from Pikeville. He defeated George Preece, a member of the Pikeville College Tennis team, 6–1, 6–0, in the final match for the second consecutive year. (Picture 5)

Lee Smith—George Preece
Singles winner—Runner up

The Winners of the Doubles Title were Sue Huffman, the wife of the late Kenneth Huffman, and Lee Smith. They defeated Eddie Blackburn, a physical education instructor and tennis coach at Pikeville College, and George Preece, 6–2, 5–7, 6–3. (Picture 6)

Smith, Sue Huffman, Davis

Every year people give contributions to the scholarship fund in memory of Kenny. He was so well loved by everyone who knew him at the college and who knew of his devotion to tennis and the college. Many of the donors from the first year are listed in the appendix. I know many others have given since then, and every one of them is greatly appreciated. It keeps the memory alive in Pikeville, Kentucky, and it encourages young people everywhere to exercise and play tennis—one of the best sports for the entire body.

By 1975, I had gone back to Morehead State University to finish my master's degree by myself with my two babies. It was much harder this time. I only lacked six hours, and I had to get these on campus. I lived in the married housing apartments close to my cousin Stephen Butcher. This seemed to make me feel safer. All the teachers were shocked when they heard about Kenny, and they were very understanding.

One day, Kenny Boy ran away from pre-school and went to the gymnasium. I had gone grocery shopping. Finally, one of the teachers called me to inform me that they had been entertaining him for two hours, and he was doing great. I don't know what I would have done without the Athletic Department at Morehead. They were like an extended family.

I finally received my master's degree. My thesis was, "A Comparison of The One-Handed Backhand Stroke and The Two-handed Backhand Stroke in Tennis Using The Variables, Power and Accuracy." I then headed back to Pikeville with my children to settle down for a short time. I was trying to get a job as a physical education teacher in the

Pikeville area or in the state of Kentucky on the college level, but it didn't work out. I eventually sent my application to other colleges and universities. One of those universities was located in Murfreesboro, Tennessee. I got the job and left for Murfreesboro late that summer.

By 1976, I couldn't play in the tournament because of my responsibilities as women's athletic director at Middle Tennessee State University, but I kept up with all of the news about the tournament that year and ever after. That year, Lee Smith was playing on the tennis team at the college with the help of the Kenneth Warren Huffman Scholarship. I was so happy the scholarship was helping him. He lost to one of his teammates, John Dotson, and came in second place. (Article 9—*Pike County News*)

PC's John Dotson captures Huffman Tennis Singles title.

John Dotson, No. 1 seeded tennis player at Pikeville, captured the Kenneth Huffman Memorial Tennis Tourney singles Wednesday night at the Huffman courts in Pikeville

Dotson defeated fellow teammate Lee Smith, 6–2, 6–3, for the championship. Dotson reached the finals

*by downing E.K. Hammond of Williamson, 6–0,
6–1. Smith dumped Russell Musick, 7–5, 6–3.*

*Doubles play also began last night with Lumpy
Newsome and Julius Layne dropping Mike Huffman
and Allen Gross, 6–2, 3–6, 6–4. Phil Glover and
Grodie Johnson defeated Karen Coleman and Doug
Goss, 6–1, 6–0; David Yarus and Gene consequently
lost to Ken Cottrell and Tim Johnson by a close 7–6
margin twice.*

*Green and Smith lost to Dotson and Victor Allara by
a 6–2, 6–0 score and Burchett and McGuire downed
Greg Spradlin and Rusty Music.* (End Article)

The tournament kept growing year after year. Granny
Huffman would send me the articles, and I kept them in a
scrapbook. I wanted to come back and play, but my health
was getting worse. People handle death differently. I took it
all inward. My grieving lasted many, many years. I developed
an illness called *fibromyalgia* (see appendix). This stopped my
tennis playing. I had to lay down my racket, but it did not
stop my love for the game. I still watched all the Grand Slams
and Master events I could find on television. If I had to go
somewhere, I would tape them.

Several years later, in Murfreesboro, Tennessee, I met
Hale Bradford Stanley one evening after a Bible study. He

knew that I loved the Lord and that I had two precious children. But he wasn't a sports fanatic like I was. My son, Kenny, loved baseball, and of course I loved tennis, so, Brad learned enough about each sport to make us happy. I married Brad in January, and I was blessed with my third child one year and eleven months later. His name is William Bradford Mason Stanley. He has been a joy to us his entire life. He also played tennis. I did manage, off and on, to hit some with all three of my children until I couldn't do it any longer. All three became good players. My daughter, Missy, and my daughter-in-law, Jacqui, both play at a high level in ALTA. Tennis will always be part of our family. After all, we started out that way.

My older children grew up like their dad, playing several sports. Kenny played baseball as his major sport, even though he was very good in basketball and tennis as well. Missy played softball as a young girl and ended up playing tennis as an adult. My son Brad played basketball because he was tall like his dad. Tennis was the one consistent sport that ran in our family. Even today, my grandchildren play tennis.

We moved to Atlanta in 1980. I've always been glad we did. It offered my children many opportunities they would never have had, especially in sports. Also, at this time in my life, I needed a change. I wanted to seek out some new doctors and get other opinions on better methods to treat my illness. Spiritually, our family needed a move because we needed to grow in the Lord. Atlanta sounded really good.

I didn't work again until 1992 when I decided to teach school. I could no longer coach or teach physical education, but I still had something to offer children. I always loved children of all ages, especially middle grades. I started teaching fifth and sixth grades in the DeKalb County School System and remained for ten years. After that I retired because of my health.

Now, I have ten grandchildren that keep me busy and as active as I can be. I try to make all their ball games and practices, if I have the energy. I have to rest and take care of myself, but when I show up I get hugs, smiles, and kisses. It is worth a million dollars. Plus, I love to watch baseball, softball, tennis, or dancing. It doesn't matter to me what they are involved in. I just want to be part of their lives.

As my life was progressing, so was the Kenneth Warren Huffman Memorial Tennis Tournament. By 1982, there were many more contributors to the scholarship fund and more participants in the tournament. The tournament was held July 31 through August 8 at the Kenneth Huffman Memorial Tennis Courts at Pikeville College. It was sponsored by the Pikeville College Alumni Association and East Kentucky

Beverage. The winner of the Men's singles was John Young of Salyersville, Kentucky, who defeated Harvey Tackett of Pikeville. Glenna Hatfield of Williamson, West Virginia, won the women's singles over Sailaja Malempati of Pikeville. The *Appalachian Express* wrote an article about the tournament. (Article 10)

Scholarship Tennis Tournament Completed at Pikeville College

The 1982 Kenneth Huffman Memorial Scholarship Tennis Tournament was held Saturday through Sunday, July 31 through August 8 at the Kenneth Huffman Memorial Tennis Courts at Pikeville College. The tournament was sponsored for the third year by the Pikeville College Alumni Association and East Kentucky Beverage, in part.

The tournament, held in memory of one of Pikeville's best tennis players, was sponsored to raise money for the Kenneth Huffman Tennis Scholarship Endowment Fund. This fund provides scholarships for students playing tennis at Pikeville College. This year's entry fees and donations totaled $1073.50.

The winner of the men's 'A' singles was John Young of Salyersville who defeated Harvey Tackett of Pikeville in the finals with a score of 6–2, 6–1.

Aaron Crum of Prestonsburg was the victor in the men's 'B' singles by downing David Spradlin of Prestonsburg, 7–5, 6–2.

Glenna Hatfield of Williamson, West Virginia took the honors in the women's singles over Sailaja Malempati of Pikeville with a final score of 7–6, 7–5.

The final match of the men's doubles was between a Prestonsburg team and a Pikeville team. Russell Music Jr. and Thomas Tackett of Prestonsburg won the event with Victor Allara and Harvey Tackett of Pikeville placing second, 6–3, 6–3.

Terry Compton and Nancy Spradlin of Prestonsburg won the title in the women's doubles by defeating Vada Huffman and Christy Bartley of Pikeville 6–3, 6–4.

The victors in the mixed doubles were Brian Marcum and Glenna Hatfield of Williamson who routed David Yarus of Pikeville and Susie Kim of Lexington, 6–2, 6–1. (End Article)

By 1986, participation in the tournament was overwhelming. There was much support again from the community. It had grown so much that it had to move to several facilities. It was played at Bob Amos Recreation Park, the Pikeville High School Complex, and the Green Meadow Country Club Tennis Courts. Again, the East Kentucky Beverage Company and the First National Bank of Pikeville co-sponsored the tournament along with the Pikeville College Alumni Association. By now there were close to one hundred participants in the tournament. Each year the entries increased. In the men's 'A' singles, Danny Wood defeated Oscar Neece. In the women's final, Linda Keeton defeated Francis Smith. The article below was published August 22, 1986 by the *Appalachian News–Express*. (Picture 7, Article 11)

Linda Keeton—Francis Smith

Linda Keeton of Paintsville (left) defeated Francis Smith of Pikeville 6–1, 6–2, to take home the women's singles title in the Kenneth Huffman Memorial Tennis Tournament at Pikeville College. (End Article)

In 1988, Lee Smith returned to play in the tournament. He was the first recipient of the Kenneth Huffman Scholarship fund. The Pikeville College paper, *The Echo*, wrote an article about his return and honored Kenny. (Picture 8, Article 12)

Huffman Recipient Returns Favor

Lee Smith

Thirteen years ago, Lee Smith ('80) attended Pikeville College on a full scholarship from the Kenneth Huffman Memorial Tennis Tournament.

Today, a successful attorney and father of two, Mr. Smith returns the favor by playing in the tournament. His entry fee each year goes into a fund which is used to provide scholarships to deserving students.

But the tournament means more to the avid tennis player; it is a way of remembering Ken Huffman, the man who helped him learn to play the game. When he began playing, at age 10, Pikeville College had the only courts in the area, and Ken Huffman, the school's tennis coach, was often there. Mr. Huffman, who was then in his late twenties, began playing tennis with him when Lee was 11.

"Ken was a gentleman on and off the court," Mr. Smith says now. "He was very patient with me, and always available for counsel."

Mr. Huffman died in 1973 of cancer, and his wife established the tournament in his honor. This year, more than 100 area tennis players participated in the event, helping students like Mr. Smith attend Pikeville College.

After he graduated, Mr. Smith earned a law degree from Chase Law School and is now an associate of the Pikeville law firm Todd & Smith. He lives in Pikeville with his wife Sandy and their children, Candice, 4, and Stephanie, 2. (End Article)

The Huffman Memorial Tennis Tournament kicked off to a good start in year 2000. The date was changed from June to August. Tournament play began on August 21 and concluded with finals on August 27 at Bob Amos Park in Pikeville. Proceeds from the tournament benefited the Pikeville College Scholarship Fund. The winners of each event are listed in the following article printed in the fall issue of the Pikeville College magazine, *The Echo*. (Article 13)

(November of 2000)

Tennis Tournament Nets Rewards for Scholarship Fund

Tennis enthusiasts took to the college courts in August, as the 27th annual Pikeville College Kenneth Huffman Memorial Tennis Tournament got under way.

The Pikeville College athletic department sponsored the week long event, which got underway Aug. 21.

Proceeds from the tournament benefited the Pikeville College Student Scholarship Fund.

Previously held in June, the tournament was moved to August this year to give players additional practice time during the summer.

Pikeville College Women's Tennis Coach Frances Coleman has been involved with the tournament for several years. Although players are competitive, Coleman said the event is a recreational tournament to many participants.

"Tennis is growing here, and there is more interest in it than there was five years ago," said Coleman. "People are now recognizing that you can play tennis at any age. It's a sport for a lifetime." (End Article)

Time goes by so fast when you're having fun. Our lives change so much.

My children are grown with children of their own playing in their own tournaments. Some tournaments are baseball, some are softball, and some are tennis. It doesn't matter. What matters is that they all enjoy playing sports. I'm very fortunate to have all of them living in the Atlanta area. That way I can watch them all play. It's a blast. One day I'm watching tennis. Then the next day I'm watching baseball. Then I'll find myself going to a ballet practice or soccer practice. I take pictures wherever I go. The following pictures (9 through 16) are my children and grandchildren posing for their favorite sport.

Coach Kenny and Kenneth
Baseball

Coach Brad and son Brad
Baseball

Missy
Tennis

Savannah
Tennis

Hannah
Softball

Ben–Soccer

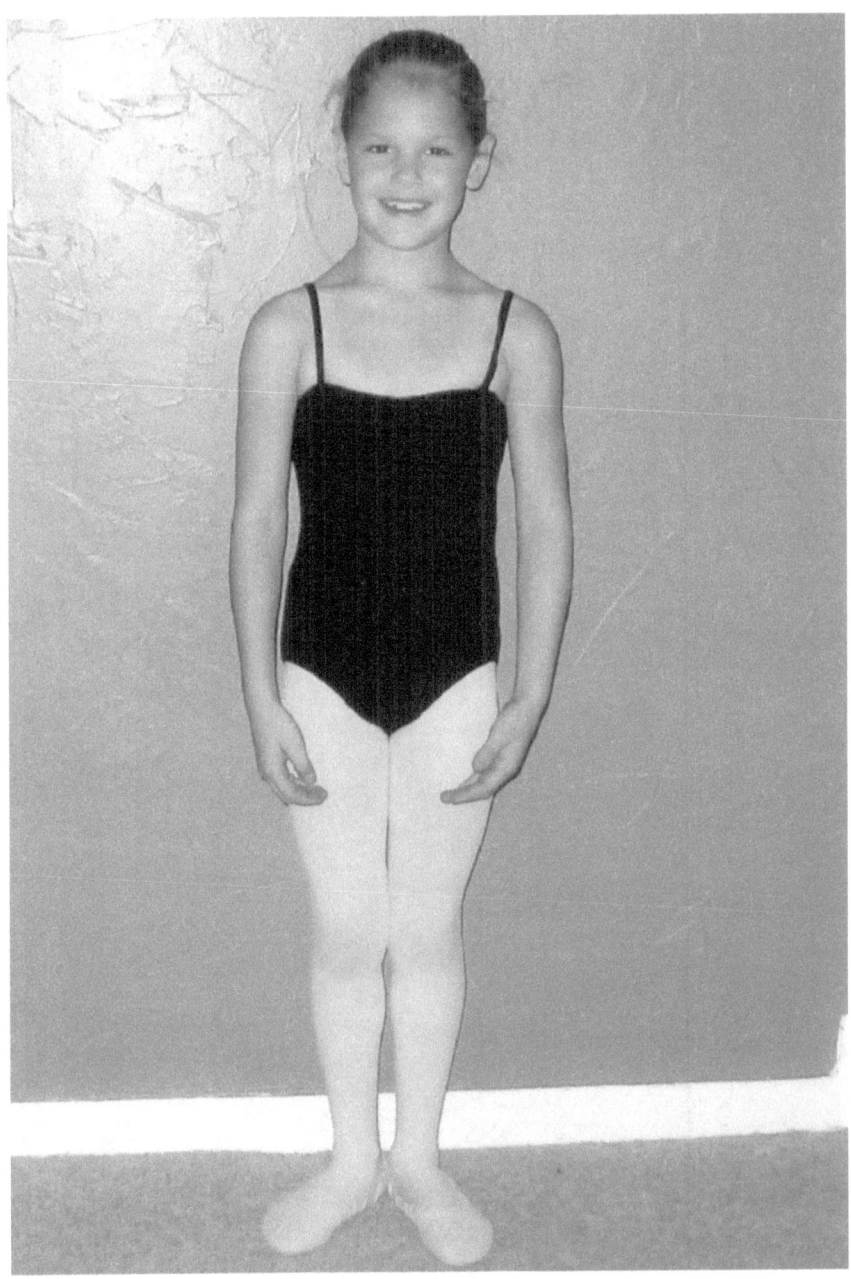

Katie
Ballet

Will
Baseball

Eventually, they will pick one or two sports they like best or in which they excel. That's the way it works. I'll be happy for them whatever they choose. I chose tennis because I love it, and I found someone who loved it as much as I did. Every time we played, it became more enjoyable, and we grew closer. I think that's the way it was meant to be: Kenny and I, going on with our lives, playing tennis, tennis, and more tennis—living our lives as long as the Lord allowed.

The tournament in 2007 was a great success. I was able to attend the tournament and give out the trophies. My husband, Brad, and I drove 350 miles from Atlanta to Pikeville, Kentucky. The trip was great. The scenery on the way was beautiful. The tournament was held at Bob Amos Park on September 22–23. The proceeds were to benefit the Pikeville College men's and women's tennis programs. It was hosted by the Pike County Tennis Association, a Mountain Tennis Circuit event. There were only fifty participants, but many talented players were present. I was especially thrilled with the quality of the play of the juniors, especially Tanner Queen, William Tan, and Donny Butcher. We met some wonderful people: parents supporting children, brothers and sisters supporting each other, and friends playing doubles. Victor Allara directed the tournament and did a great job. The tournament had over seven different divisions.

The tennis results were as follows:

The Women's Singles event was won by Suzanne Preece by a score of 6–2, 6–2. She ran her opponent back and forth on the court, working her very hard. The match was closer than it looked, but Suzanne came out victorious.

Women's Singles

Champion Suzanne Preece

The Men's Singles event was won by Cary Brand by a score of 6–4, 7–6. The runner-up was Ronnie Stapleton. Both players had a lot of skill. It was enjoyable to watch them pounding the ball back and forth. (Picture 17)

Men's Singles

Champion—Cary Brand
Runner up—Ronnie Stapleton

Trophies presented by
Sue Huffman Stanley

The Men's Doubles event was won by Ron Compton and Steve Huffman, Kenny's brother. I was very proud of him. The score was 6–1, 6–2. They had to play some much younger players and still came away victorious.

Men's Doubles

Champions Steve Huffman and Ron Compton

Trophy presentation by
Sue Huffman Stanley

The Men's Senior Singles was won by Truman Fields by a score of 6–3, 6–2. The runner-up was Ralph Hood.

Men's Senior Singles

Champion–Truman Fields
Runner-up–Ralph Hood

In the younger divisions, the Eighteen and Under Girls Singles was won by Hayley Kincaid with a score of 6–0, 6–1. The runner-up was Courtney Gullett. (Picture 20)

Eighteen and Under Girls Singles

Champion–Hayley Kincaid
Runner-up–Courtney Gullett

Trophies presented by
Sue Huffman Stanley

The Eighteen and Under Boys was won by William Tan by a score of 6–2, 6–1. The runner-up was Tanner Queen.

Eighteen and Under Boys

Champion–William Tan

Trophy presented by
Sue Huffman Stanley

The Twelve and Under Boys was won by Alex Rosadio by a score of 6–0, 6–1.

Twelve and Under Boys

Champion—Alex Rosadio

Trophy presented by
Sue Huffman Stanley

I expect to be back next year and give out the trophies again. It was a wonderful tournament with a lot of talent. We hope for even more talent next year. Tennis had gone down in the area since the nineties, but it's coming up again.

Anytime you see a kid or a young person, stick a racket in their hand. Hire a couple of coaches at your local YMCA. Pour a little money into your area, and get the kids off the streets. I want Pikeville to be the center of tennis for eastern Kentucky again like it was in the eighties and nineties. Give these young people a chance. We expect big things to happen in the future. Maybe we can add more tennis courts and bleachers so parents can watch their children play.

At the tennis courts hangs a sign: "Kenneth Warren Huffman Memorial Tennis Courts." (Picture 23)

At present, I am sixty years old. I live in Tucker, Georgia. My three children, ten grandchildren, and my husband and I are very happy. I've gone through much suffering in my life, especially by losing Kenny when we were so young. I thought my life was over, but by the Lord's mercy and love, He brought me through it all. He was faithful and put joy back into my life.

At times, my life has been very complicated—like when I had both feet operated on at the same time or when I broke both ankles at the age of fifty-five, just six weeks apart from each other. I seem to do everything full-force just like I used to play tennis. I don't know any other way. So, if I love someone, I love with all my heart.

God has been very faithful to me. I have been surrounded with people who have loved me my entire life, and now that I am sixty, I'm the most blessed woman on earth. My husband tells me that he loves me every day. My children call me all the time, and my grandchildren are always giving me hugs and kisses. Pictures 23 through 26 show my children and their families and Brad and me like we are today.

From left to right

Kenny, Kenneth, Jacqui, Ryan

Top row: Jon, Missy

Bottom row: Hannah, Ben

Top row
Brad, Savannah

Middle row
Christa, Brad, Katie

Bottom row
Joe–on Mom's lap

Boaz–between Dad's legs
Will–holding on with both hands

Brad and I

Granny Huffman is still like a second mother to me. My mother is still alive and doing well in Pikeville, Kentucky. My sisters, of course, have grandchildren of their own to take care of, but we are very close and visit each other every chance we get. I have many wonderful Christian friends that I get to be with often. Life is much simpler now, not so complicated.

The love of my life today is the Lord. Everything else fits into place. I still love tennis as much as I did. I don't get to play it, but I sure do love watching it. I just finished watching Pete Sampras play again on the Champion Circuit, the Senior Tour. I never thought I'd get to watch him play again. It thrilled my heart. Many times I prefer to watch Pete or Jim

Courier play because they were the ones I enjoyed watching so much. They were in that group I call the "Fabulous Five" that America was so proud of. I think we have another group coming up soon. Whether they will be as good or not we will just have to wait and see.

As for tennis, time changes, but the game doesn't change much. I was glad to see tennis add the challenge replay to some of the Grand Slams in 2007. I thought it improved the game. I know it made it more interesting to the fans. I'm not sure about bringing coaching to the court. Maybe I'm a little old-fashioned. I'll leave that up to the players to decide.

I'm sure another thing the players might like is a shorter season. Of course, for the fans, they would want tennis year 'round, but pretty soon your body wears down and it needs some recuperation. When I was playing, we couldn't play all four seasons because of the weather. We played from March until October. Then we had to stop due to cold temperatures and snow. Today the pros travel to sites all over the world. It must be very difficult on their bodies. I'm sure that eventually something will be done about the scheduling. Any way you put it, TENNIS is a wonderful sport. I fell in love with it when I was thirteen years old and at the same time I fell in love with Kenny. He left me two wonderful children and several grandchildren whom I adore. He also gave me love for a sport that I will have with me until the day I die. But the most important thing he left with me was his testimony of how much he loved the Lord. That is the most lasting thing. He was a good man, a wonderful dad and husband, and a super tennis player—and I loved him dearly.

The End

APPENDIX

Kenneth Warren Huffman

(1944–1973)

Kenny was the son of William Milton Huffman and Eleanor Huffman. He had one brother, Steve. He went to Pikeville High School, graduated from Pikeville College, and was a member of the First Baptist Church. He worked at the First National Bank when he died. Kenny played tennis in the Pikeville area from age sixteen to the age of twenty-eight. He won practically every tournament he entered. He was a member of the Pikeville College Tennis team. He was the father of Kenneth Warren Huffman II and Susan Melissa Huffman. The tennis courts at the college are named after Kenny due to his influence on tennis in the area. A scholarship was started in his name at the college, and a tournament is held every year in his memory. He was married to the former Sue Butcher.

The Kenneth Warren Huffman Memorial Scholarships

The scholarship was started in 1973 in memory of Kenny Huffman, one of the best tennis players to ever play in the Pikeville area. The scholarship fund helps recruit tennis players for Pikeville College and helps provide them with a good education. The scholarship is funded by contributions given by donors and by entry fees into the Kenneth Warren Huffman Memorial Tennis Tournament. Many of the donors from the first year include:

Dr. N.A. Chrisman, Sr.

Dr. G.N. Combs

Mrs. Harding Dawahare

Mrs. Adron Doron

Mrs. Pearl R. Gerard

Mr. and Mrs. William Huffman

Mr. Douglas Mack Justice

Mr. Jack T. Page

Mr. James E. Rogers

Mr. Lon B. Rogers

Ms. May E. Shurtleff

Mr. Walter P. Walters, Sr.

Mr. Michael Williamson

If you would like to contribute to the scholarship fund, contact the Athletic Department at Pikeville College. The phone number is: 606-218-5250

The Kenneth Warren Huffman
Memorial Tennis Tournament

This tournament was started in 1973 in memory of Kenny Huffman. It has continued annually all of these years, with the exception of two or three years when circumstances beyond our control prevented the tournament from taking place. Tennis players come from all over eastern Kentucky and surrounding states to play in the tournament. It has had as many as 100 participants. Last year (2007) there were fifty participants and seven different divisions. All fees from the tournament go to the Pikeville College Scholarship Fund. Each year trophies and tee shirts are given out at the end of the tournament. Every year stronger and better talent participates. In 2008, a few ranked players in the state of Kentucky played in the tournament. If you would like to help sponsor the *Kenneth Warren Huffman Memorial Tennis Tournament*, e-mail Sue Huffman Stanley at KWHMTT@gmail.com.

Children and Grandchildren

I have three children—Kenneth Warren Huffman II, Susan Melissa Huffman Dasher, and William Bradford Mason Stanley. Kenny is a financial analyst for a company in Atlanta. Missy was an accountant and is now a homemaker. Brad is a chemical engineer.

I have been blessed with ten grandchildren. Their names are:

Kenneth Warren Huffman III

Ryan Matthew Huffman

Hannah Melissa Dasher

Benjamin Paul Dasher

Savannah Rachel Stanley

Katherine Rebecca Stanley

Paul Bradford Stanley

William Benjamin Stanley

Adam Boaz Stanley

Joe Asher Stanley

Fibromyalgia

Fibromyalgia is a condition characterized by widespread pain in the muscles, ligaments, and tendons. A person may not have any energy and may have trouble sleeping. It is considered a long-lasting, chronic condition with no cure. For more information, please see the following website: *http://www.revolutionhealth.com/conditions/bones-joints-muscles/*

www.ingramcontent.com/pod-product-compliance
Lightning Source LLC
Chambersburg PA
CBHW031230280526
45784CB00004B/1515

* 9 7 8 1 4 3 8 9 3 2 3 2 3 *